PETS' GUIDES

Gordon's Guide to

Caring for Your Guinea Pigs

Isabel Thomas

Heinemann
LIBRARY

Chicago, Illinois

Edited by James Benefield and Brynn Baker
Designed by Cynthia Akiyoshi
Picture research by Tracy Cummins
Production by Victoria Fitzgerald
Originated by Capstone Global Library Ltd
Printed and bound in China by RR Donnelley Asia

18 17 16 15 14
10 9 8 7 6 5 4 3 2 1

Library of Congress Cataloging-in-Publication Data
Thomas, Isabel, 1979- author.
    Gordon's guide to caring for your guinea pigs
/ Isabel Thomas.
        pages cm.—(Pets' guides)
    Summary: "In this book, Gordon the Guinea
Pig reveals how readers should go about
choosing pet guinea pigs, what supplies they will
need, how to make a new pet guinea pig feel at
home, and how to properly care for pet guinea
pigs, including feeding, exercising, and keeping
a guinea pig cage clean. Text is accompanied
by clear, labeled photographs to further reinforce
key concepts, and the use of an animal narrator
also allows the book to be used to teach
perspective"—Provided by publisher.

    Includes bibliographical references
and index.

ISBN 978-1-4846-0261-4 (hardcover)
ISBN 978-1-4846-0268-3 (paperback)
ISBN 978-1-4846-0284-3 (eBook PDF)
1. Guinea pigs as pets—Juvenile literature.
I. Title.
    SF459.G9
    636.935'92—dc23   2013040450

Acknowledgments
We would like to thank the following for
permission to reproduce photographs:
Alamy: © blickwinkel, 26, © KARL REDSHAW, 14;
Biosphoto: J.-L. Klein & M.-L. Hubert, front cover;
Capstone Library: Karon Dubke, 5, 11, 21; Getty
Images: kickers, 8, 13, Vstock LLC, 17, Yellow Dog
Productions, 7; Glow Images: Arco Images/
GmbH/Wegner, 19; Shutterstock: Monkey Business
Images, 24; Superstock: Juniors, 22; Design
Elements Shutterstock: iBird, Picsfive, R-studio

We would like to thank Faye and Gary Taylor for
their assistance in the preparation of this book.

Every effort has been made to contact copyright
holders of material reproduced in this book. Any
omissions will be rectified in subsequent printings
if notice is given to the publisher.

All the Internet addresses (URLs) given in this
book were valid at the time of going to press.
However, due to the dynamic nature of the
Internet, some addresses may have changed, or
sites may have changed or ceased to exist since
publication. While the author and publisher regret
any inconvenience this may cause readers,
no responsibility for any such changes can be
accepted by either the author or the publisher

Contents

Do You Want Pet Guinea Pigs? 4

Choosing Your Guinea Pigs 6

Getting Ready 10

Welcome Home. 12

Feeding Time 14

Handling 16

Playtime 18

Cleaning My Home. 20

Grooming and Tooth Care 22

Visiting the Vet 24

Vacation Care. 26

Guinea Pig Facts. 28

Gordon's Top Tips. 29

Glossary. 30

Find Out More 31

Index 32

Some words are shown in bold, **like this**. You can find out what they mean by looking in the glossary.

Do You Want Pet Guinea Pigs?

Squeak! I'm Gordon and this book is all about guinea pigs like me. Guinea pigs aren't really pigs, we're **rodents**. We make great pets. We are calm and friendly and love being with our favorite humans.

Before giving a home to guinea pigs, be sure you can look after us properly. We'll need food, water, and a clean place to live. Plus, we need company, safe toys to play with, and **vet** care if we get sick or injured.

Choosing Your Guinea Pigs

Which type of guinea pig would suit your family? Smooth-coated guinea pigs like me have short fur. We are easy to care for! If you choose a long-haired or rough-coated guinea pig, you will need to become an expert at brushing guinea pig hair.

Animal shelters and **rescue centers** are the best places to find guinea pigs. You could also adopt guinea pigs from a good **breeder**, or buy them from a pet store. Visit the guinea pigs first to make sure they are happy and healthy.

I get very lonely when I'm on my own. Guinea pigs like to live in small groups, so you will need to get at least two. Choose girl guinea pigs or boy guinea pigs.

If you would like to keep boy guinea pigs, it is best to get two brothers. Otherwise, the boy guinea pigs might fight! Getting all boy or all girl guinea pigs prevents unwanted baby guinea pigs.

Getting Ready

Now it's time to shop for everything your new guinea pig needs. First on the list is a home big enough to run around and explore. Also make sure it's tall, so I can stand up on my back legs without bumping my head.

Fill my home with places to hide, tunnels to play in, rocks to climb, and wooden toys to chew. Don't forget the bedroom! A clay flowerpot will do. I like to nibble everything, so even the bedding should be safe to eat.

Welcome Home

We can live outdoors if the temperature is 59 degrees Fahrenheit (15 degrees Celsius) or warmer. If it gets colder than this where you live, keep me indoors. If I get too hot I can get very sick, so keep my cage away from sunny windows, radiators, and heaters. Also, keep us away from direct sunlight.

The perfect spot for my new home is:

- quiet and calm
- protected from drafts. I like lots of space for warm bedding too!
- away from other pets. I'm scared of cats and dogs!
- always between 59-68 degrees Fahrenheit (15-20 degrees Celsius)
- somewhere I won't disturb you at night

Feeding Time

I like to nibble hay and drink water all day long. Give me guinea pig pellets every morning and evening. These are made from plants, seeds, and vegetables, with plenty of a special chemical called Vitamin C to keep me healthy.

Don't forget the snacks! Leafy green vegetables will make me a happy and healthy guinea pig. You can even give me fresh grass and dandelion leaves from the yard. Yum!

Handling

Spend time with me every day. At first I may freeze or hide if I'm feeling scared. Be quiet and gentle. Offer me treats, such as small pieces of a carrot or an apple, to show me that you are friendly and safe.

Pick me up safely by supporting my bottom with one hand, and hold me close to your chest. Sit down when you are handling me, so I don't get hurt if I wriggle out of your hands. Stroke me gently and I might even purr.

Playtime

Once I've settled in, please let me play outside my cage every day. Create a safe space with places to hide. Watch me carefully to make sure I don't escape or get into trouble. I like to chew everything and I don't know what is dangerous.

Put some exciting toys in my cage, so I can keep playing when you're asleep or at school. Plastic pipes and large cardboard tubes make good tunnels. Rocks and ramps are fun to climb. Deep piles of hay are great for digging.

Cleaning My Home

A good guinea pig owner has jobs to do every day. Change my water and clear away any leftover pellets or fresh food. Take out any damp bedding and droppings. Once a week, give my whole cage a full cleaning.

Gordon's cleaning tips:

- 🐾 clear out the dirty bedding
- 🐾 scrub my cage floor with warm water and a **disinfectant**
- 🐾 remember to wash my toys and hiding places, too
- 🐾 let everything dry
- 🐾 fill my cage with fresh, clean bedding

Grooming and Tooth Care

While you are busy keeping my cage clean, I'm busy **grooming** myself. Help me keep my fur clean and shiny by brushing me with a special soft brush. If you have long-haired guinea pigs, you'll need to do this every day.

Like all rodents, my teeth never stop growing.
I stop them from getting too long by **gnawing**
on wood. They don't overgrow often, but
please make sure I always have branches,
twigs, or unpainted wooden toys.

Visiting the Vet

Take your guinea pigs to visit a vet every year.
Go back if we get ill between check-ups.
Guinea pigs are not very good at showing
you when they're sick or injured.

Look out for these signs that I need to visit a vet:

- my teeth are getting too long
- I'm coughing, sneezing, or **wheezing**
- I'm not playing or moving, or I am hiding more than normal
- I have diarrhea or a dirty bottom
- I'm doing fewer droppings than usual
- I'm not grooming myself or my skin looks strange or lumpy
- you spot any **mites** or **worms** on my body or in my droppings
- I become thin very quickly

Vacation Care

If you go on vacation, find someone to look after me while you're away. Tell them how to change my food and water, keep my cage clean, and help me exercise. Give them the list of signs I show if I need to visit a vet.

Moving can be scary for guinea pigs.
If I have to stay in a different place while
you're away, take my toys along, too. The
smell will remind me of home.

Guinea Pig Facts

- Guinea pigs are also called "cavies."

- Guinea pigs don't need much sleep. They eat, play, and explore day and night.

- Guinea pigs make lots of different noises. They "wheek" when excited, "chutt" when exploring, and "purr" when handled.

- Guinea pigs usually live four to seven years.

Gordon's Top Tips

- Make my cage as large as possible, with lots of space to run around. Fill it with plenty of things to see and do.

- Don't worry if you see me eating my droppings. This is how I get all the goodness out of the food!

- You can teach guinea pigs to go to the toilet in a litter box.

- When cleaning my cage, use vinegar and an old toothbrush to get rid of crusty stains.

Glossary

animal shelter organization that cares for animals that do not have homes

breeder person who helps animals to have babies in an organized way

disinfectant chemicals used to clean and kill germs

gnaw bite or chew something again and again

groom clean an animal's fur or skin

mite tiny spider-like insect that lives on larger animals

rescue center organization that rescues animals that are lost, injured, or not being taken care of properly

rodent type of animal with front teeth that never stop growing, such as guinea pigs

vet person trained to care for ill and injured animals

wheezing breathing with a whistling or rattling sound

worm tiny animal that lives inside other animals and can make them ill

Find Out More

Books

Bearce, Stephanie. *Care* for a Pet Guinea Pig.
Hockessin, Del.: Mitchell Lane Publishers, 2010.

Ganeri, Anita. *Guinea Pigs* (A Pet's Life).
Heinemann-Raintree, 2009.

Websites

Learn more about guinea pigs at:
http://aspca.org/pet-care/small-pet-care/guinea-pig-care

Discover more about guinea pigs at:
http://humanesociety.org/animals/guinea_pigs

Index

animal shelters 7

breeders 7

droppings 20, 25, 29

food 5, 14, 15, 16, 20, 26, 29

fur 6, 22

groups 8

handling 16, 17

housing 5, 10, 11, 12, 13, 19, 20, 21, 26, 29

noises 28

outdoors 12

pet stores 7

rescue centers 7

teeth 23, 25

toys 5, 11, 19, 21, 23, 27

vets 5, 24, 25

water 5, 14, 20, 21, 26